BOND ON SET

**FILMING
QUANTUM OF SOLACE
GREG WILLIAMS**

007

LONDON, NEW YORK, MUNICH,
MELBOURNE, and DELHI

Art Direction and Design Mike Bone
Senior Editor Alastair Dougall
Brand Manager Lisa Lanzarini
Publishing Manager Simon Beecroft
Category Publisher Alex Allan
Production Amy Bennett
Production Editor Sean Daly

First published in Great Britain in 2008 by Dorling Kindersley Limited,
80 Strand, London WC2R 0RL

A Penguin Company

06 07 08 09 10 10 9 8 7 6 5 4 3 2 1

A CIP catalogue record for this book is available from the British Library.

ISBN: 978-1-40533-259-0

Colour reproduction by Alta Image, London
Printed and bound in Slovakia by TBB spol. s r.o., Banska Bystrica

See our complete catalogue at
www.dk.com

FOREWORD
Michael G. Wilson
Barbara Broccoli

This is Greg Williams' third "Bond On Set" book and his fourth James Bond film and, thus, by any measure Greg is a Bond veteran and a well-loved member of the Bond family. His success is due in large part to a professional, no-nonsense approach to each assignment, a consequence of his early career as a photojournalist. From the age of nineteen, Greg accepted tough assignments in world trouble spots such as Burma, Chechnya, and Sierra Leone. He also tackled emotionally challenging assignments such as documenting a young woman's death from CJD (the human form of Mad Cow Disease), Thalidomide's second generation of deformed children, and the rehabilitation of brain-injured children. One would have thought that after mastering such demanding assignments working around a film set would be fairly easy. But Greg has found film assignments have their own unique problems that are far from simple.

For Greg, QUANTUM OF SOLACE was not so much about forging new relationships, as expanding his role beyond reportage. He undertook a myriad of special advertising, poster, and editorial assignments for virtually every member of the cast. To do this he had to discard his normal, low profile, "fly-on-the-wall" style and instead assert himself to get the shots he needed. The demands of the film and the volume of studio work in London necessitated relocation of him and his family from New York to the UK.

It has been a pleasure to see how well Greg has done in the past ten years we have known him. His personal and professional life has prospered. He and Sarah are married, and have a beautiful daughter, Peggy. He is in great demand both inside and outside the film world as a photographer of distinction for portraiture, fashion, editorial, and advertising. But he has not gone soft; he still enjoys dangerous assignments with his brother, Olly, photographing "interactions" with the world's greatest predators in remote regions of the world. Just last year he went with artists Olly and Suzi on a dog-sled trek in the Arctic to flush out polar bears... could this mission have been preparation for his work with film stars?

INTRODUCTION
Marc Forster

It's a cold and rainy morning in July. I'm in London. It's been three weeks since we wrapped production. Strolling down memory lane always makes me feel like I'm watching a shadow of my former self, flickering against the silly notion of nostalgia. I reflect on all that has happened since I first met Barbara Broccoli and Michael Wilson last spring. It has been like a collection of pinup drawings which all form the experience of an intense journey where gravity ceases to exist. From our very first meeting at the Danjaq offices in Santa Monica, California, where I had no interest in directing the film, to being on a plane heading for Italy a month later, to the fact I actually agreed to direct the film, is one big memory lapse. Maybe it was a quote from Orson Welles who, when asked what was his greatest regret in life, said, "That I never directed a commercial film." Or maybe it was the challenge of having all odds against me that made me do it. It is those challenges that seem silly in the grand scope of life, but never fail to make my blood rush towards my temples. It is in those challenges that life always seems magnified, as if in a room of light and dark.

What I do remember, very clearly, however, is travelling on that plane, and thinking: "What kind of impression would it make if I pulled out of the movie right here and now?" My mind kept answering itself, "I'm sure Barbara and Michael would understand — we could make a short little statement to the press and underline that it was an amicable split." More thoughts sprung to mind like, "There is really no upside for me to make this movie" and "When is the best time to tell them that I'm going to pull out?" But In the brief time I had spent with Barbara and Michael, I had really enjoyed their company and I didn't want to let them down. I felt the need to follow through. My mind became a circus of inner conflict with no convictions either way.

Finally a few minutes before that plane to Italy touched down, unable to sleep all night with my eyes glued to the window, a voice echoed from within and said, "What is it that scares you? Just be relaxed and peaceful. Direct the film and be thankful for the opportunity which you've been given." One last time I let my mind race back and forth and I had one last fleeting moment of worry. I was lost for a moment, but eventually I let it all pass. I stepped out of the way of all reason and handed over the reins to my intuition, which started to guide me and help me create the vision for QUANTUM OF SOLACE.

After I committed my heart, it became all about the creative source, progressing along with my vision, and trying to find the flow within. Some directors like to create out of conflict. I need to create out of unity because, for me, that is where the flow exists. For that effort, and for their ferocity and passion, I would like to thank all my creative partners who have helped me form this film. As Confucius said, "A journey of a thousand miles begins with a single step."

Looking back, I'm thankful I dared to take this step, and I'm grateful for the opportunity which made me take it. For that, I would like to thank Barbara Broccoli and Michael Wilson — it has truly been a pleasure. I would also like to thank everyone who worked so hard, both in front of and behind the camera, for all their efforts.

Marc Forster
London, England
July 2008

PRE-PRODUCTION

Above and below: Daniel Craig puts an Aston Martin through its paces at Millbrook Proving Ground, Bedfordshire, England, in preparation for Bond's car chase in the film's opening scenes.

Above and below: On Horley Lake, Surrey, Daniel Craig familiarizes himself with the controls of a jet-powered speedboat. Craig put in hours of practice to ensure the film's boat chase (filmed in Panama, set in Haiti) looked totally convincing. Below right: Craig with 2nd unit director Dan Bradley.

Pages 14 and 15: The boat-chase stunt team rehearses.

Pages 16 and 17: The crew film Daniel Craig in Bodyflight's wind tunnel, Bedfordshire.

Page 18: Olga Kurylenko (Camille) joins Daniel Craig in a rehearsal of their free-fall over the Bolivian desert.

Page 19: Daniel Craig rehearses with his stunt double Ben Cooke.

Pre-production is the time in which the picture is suspended inside a shell, when one tries to hear the humming of images not yet born. The humming can come in many different ways and there is no recipe in knowing or finding the right tone. I'm never sure if I'm imagining it all or if it's all imagining me.

Often I lay dreaming at night, with a pen next to me, ready to write down whatever comes to mind when those images — often as textures, colours and rhythms — float into space. I always listen intently for those sounds, even if, sometimes, they're silent.

On QUANTUM OF SOLACE, the preproduction period was more important for me than on any other film I have done. Not only for the obvious reasons — shooting in multiple countries, action rehearsals, complicated visual effects, etc — but to truly understand the essence of Ian Fleming's Bond. The more I listened and heard, the more I connected with the core of Bond's character. From there on, I started to close

my eyes and imagine his struggles, his pain, his isolation, his memories and, most of all, his vision of the world. I felt as if I had been transported into Bond's world. I became inspired to create something that paid homage to the history of the franchise while simultaneously molding it to my own vision.

The most challenging part was the fact that there was not a finished script when we began. In order to keep the project moving ahead, we were scouting the world and searching for locations without knowing what it was we were really looking for. We were following hunches and speculating what could work as a location in a hypothetical story. All along, I kept wondering, "How long do the roots remain after a tree falls?" Fortunately for all of us, the tree never fell. Instead, it kept growing.

Marc Forster

Pages 22, 23, and opposite: Daniel Craig in a DBS shell attached to a go-cam. Hydraulics allow the shell to pitch realistically from side to side, while the film crew at the back drive the go-cam vehicle and capture the shell's movements.

Above, bottom right: Producer Barbara Broccoli with stunt coordinator Gary Powell and Daniel Craig.

January 28 to February 2: It was our fourth week of shooting and we were on the 007 Stage at Pinewood Studios. The sequence begins with Bond throwing Mr White down onto a chair where he is attended to by a medic. Bond then walks off and enters an anteroom above which an exposition scene between M and Bond plays out. They both return to White and proceed to interrogate him, which turns into the chase, and leads us to the Palio.

Stages always smell like dust. They are dark, uncomfortable places to work in, and I usually get a little depressed in them. I can never shake the constant feeling of being wedged against wood, nails and screws, which facilitate the endless amounts of dust. I actually believe it's the air more then anything that bothers me. I much prefer shooting on location, being in touch with a space that has lived. Locations always make me feel calm and provide me with more inspiration.

On a stage, I feel myself longing for the scent and sounds of the outside world. Sometimes when I entered the stage in the morning, I would have trouble doing so. My mind would race through the story beats that would aid me in expressing to my collaborators all that cannot be written on the page.

When people read a script or a book they always see it through their own eyes. When you're directing a movie, the thousands of eyes have to become just one pair. There are many different paths to achieve that unity, and there is no right or wrong way in one's journey, although, for me, some are harder then others. Ultimately, I let an invisible hand guide me through the experience.

Marc Forster

Pages 26 and 27: Marc Forster directs on the MI6 safe house set.

Opposite page: Daniel Craig, Judi Dench and Jesper Christensen filming the interrogation of Mr White.

Below: Shooting the scene in which Bond confronts Mitchell (Glenn Foster).

Pages 30 and 31: Judi Dench as M.

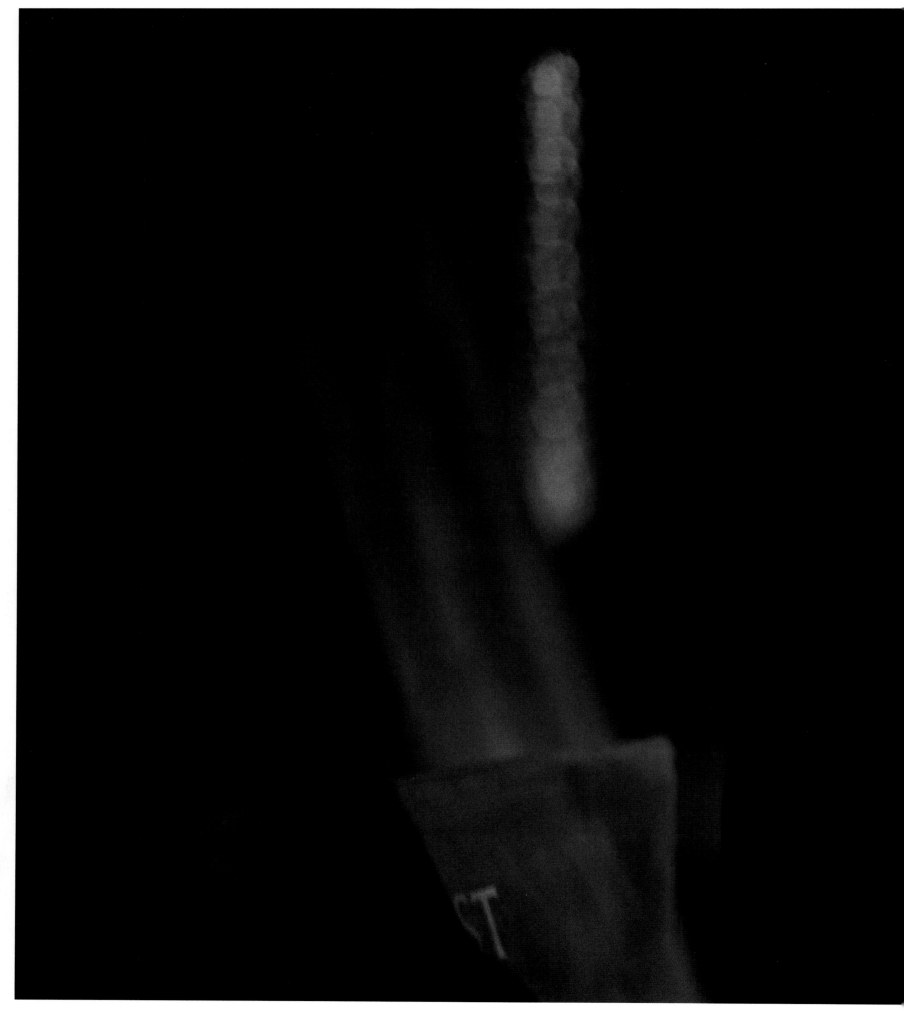

Above and opposite page: Filming Bond and
Mitchell's chase through Siena's famous Cisterns,
the city's irrigation system — recreated on the 007
stage at Pinewood.

SIENA ITALY

Pages 34, 35, above and opposite page: Filming
Bond and Mitchell's chase across the rooftops.

The roof chase was, for me, one of the most important elements in the opening beat of the film. But it was a struggle to maintain as we faced certain budgetary concerns, and I was constantly confronted with the threat and pressure of having to cut it. Originally, we planned to build the rooftops as an entire street set at Pinewood Studios, but after ordering thousands of roof tiles, we had to abandon that idea due to cost. We were extremely fortunate that the city of Siena gave us permission to shoot on top of the real roofs. At the time, this seemed like a worst-case scenario, but it actually worked out for the best. I'm still curious to know what happened to the thousands of tiles we ordered. I must look into that after I finish my notes for this book.

The next hurdle in the chase was the bus-jump element. Again, there was a discussion about whether or not to cut it for budgetary reasons. I felt the bus was a necessary story point because without it, we couldn't work out a logical way for Bond to cross over the street to Mitchell — unless the bus transported him. Somehow it all worked out for the best, and the scene has an aroma reminiscent of those 60s and 70s thrillers I love so much.

Originally, Mitchell and Bond entered the dome of the art gallery from the bottom and were fighting their way to the top. I thought it would be more spectacular if they were to crash into the dome from above. My visit to Siena and the tour of the cisterns in the belly of the city gave me the vision to start the chase underground, inter-cutting with the horse race above. As Bond and Mitchell appear in the centre of the square, they are thrust up into the crowd as the horses are crossing the finish line, juxtaposing their almost isolated world with the chaos from above.

Marc Forster

Opposite page: Daniel Craig up on the roof with the 2nd unit crew; 2nd unit director Dan Bradley (bottom right).

Above left: Craig looks on as his stunt double Bobby Holland Hanton performs a jump.

Above right: Daniel Craig performs the stunt himself.

BARBICAN, LONDON
ENGLAND

Pages 40 and 41: Rory Kinnear (Bill Tanner) and Judi Dench (M) film a scene outside the Barbican.

Above (left to right): Standby art director Peter James, 1st assistant director Michael Lerman, director of photography Roberto Schaefer, and director Marc Forster.

Thursday, January 3, was our first day of shooting. As the weeks raced by leading to this moment, I'd had a nagging feeling that we hadn't had enough time to prep the film properly. But now, today, the sand has finally rushed through the glass and there's no more time. From now on, decisions have to be made instantly, from moment to moment.

I could have played this entire scene on stage at the MI6 office set as originally planned and saved the production some money, but it was crucial for me to find an interesting exterior location for this scene. It was vital to the story to show M and Tanner out of their safety zone (the office) and in architectural surroundings that would make a visual statement about M. The location gave me the opportunity to make the characters part of something larger, but also enabled me to show the contrast between M and Bond in Haiti, conveying an image of a modern clinical environment versus one of developing-world humanity.

Once shooting begins, all lingering angst is forced to disappear and the movie starts playing and replaying over and over in my mind. I remember a few films back, my first day of shooting felt like my guts were being ripped out with a plastic fork — a pain I have since avoided. One day I realized it would be much healthier to function with a more meditative approach by understanding that ultimately everything is an illusion and that imperfection is not only unavoidable but, in fact, necessary to the final product.

Marc Forster

BREGENZ AUSTRIA

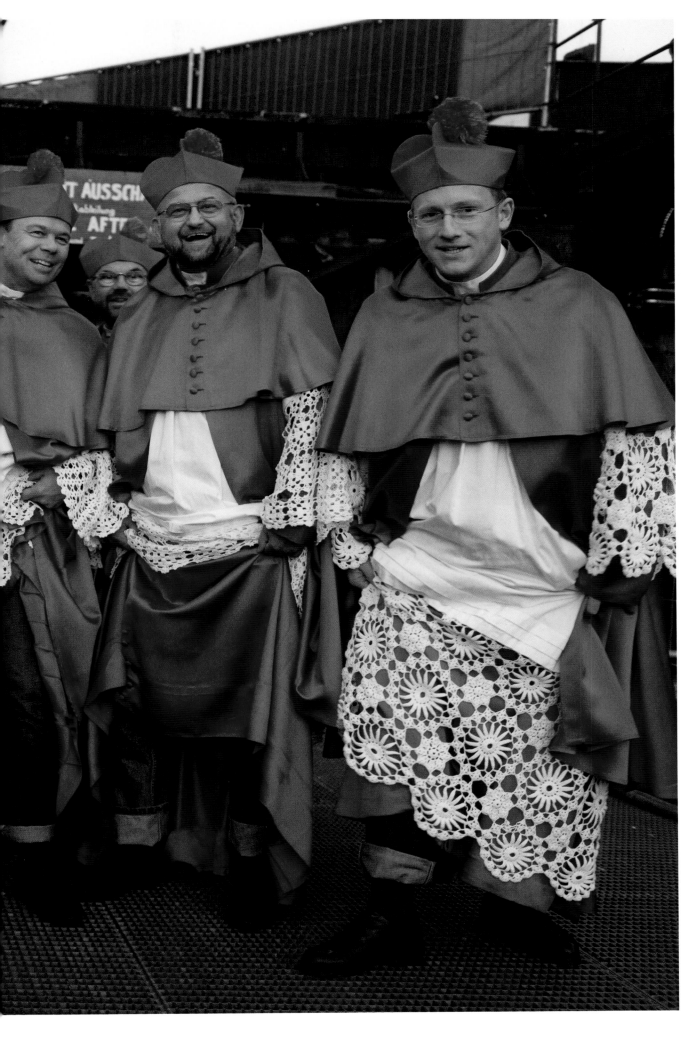

Pages 44 and 45: Dominic Greene and his henchmen. Left to right: Anatole Taubman, Carl Von Malaise, Mathieu Amalric, Thomas Bloem, Diz Sharpe.

Page 46: The magnificent stage set for Puccini's Tosca at the Festspielhaus, Bregenz.

Page 47: Mathieu Amalric as ruthless business mogul Dominic Greene, CEO of Greene Planet.

Left: Members of the cast of the production of Tosca staged at Bregenz.

Above and opposite page: Filming the chase scene through the opera house restaurant involving Bond and Dominic Greene's men. The unfortunate waiter, played by first assistant director Michael Lerman, has just caught a stray bullet in the backside! "A" camera operator George Richmond, EPK cameraman Sean Hill, and director of photography Roberto Schaefer (bottom centre) take delight in watching the footage.

Opera makes me feel as if I'm dreaming with my eyes open. Our brief time here is about trying to find our song, in which, ultimately, we all share the same one. We need to find the courage and the strength to live a sacred existence in the most conscious way. For me it has always been communicating to others through stories.

Having two stories told simultaneously in the same frame, reflecting one another, is a gift I've been given with TOSCA in Bregenz. TOSCA is a terrific metaphor for Bond on so many levels. The idea of "being watched" is revealed in such a simple way that it never draws attention to itself. The centre of the eye, which is itself being watched by the audience, is parallel to Bond as he spies on Greene and the other members of Quantum. The action between Bond and what's happening on stage go hand in hand.

It was a real challenge to shoot these scenes in the time permitted, even with two units shooting simultaneously — the main unit and an insert unit shooting right behind us. To keep the style consistent meant a lot of running back and forth between the two. The temperature would drop through the night, and the poor extras, dressed in formal eveningwear, were freezing by the lake. At least we had some good fortune: it had poured for a few weeks prior to our arrival, but never rained once during the entire period we were in Bregenz shooting.

Marc Forster

Above and opposite: Anatole Taubman and 2nd assistant director Toby Hefferman play indoor football (with a ball of gaffer tape – not pictured) during a break in filming.

Above, clockwise from top left: Daniel Craig confers with director Marc Forster, shares a joke with stunt double Ben Cooke, relaxes during a break, and in character as James Bond.

Opposite page: Daniel Craig with his stunt double Ben Cooke, assistant stunt coordinator Rob Inch, and script supervisor Nicki Clapp.

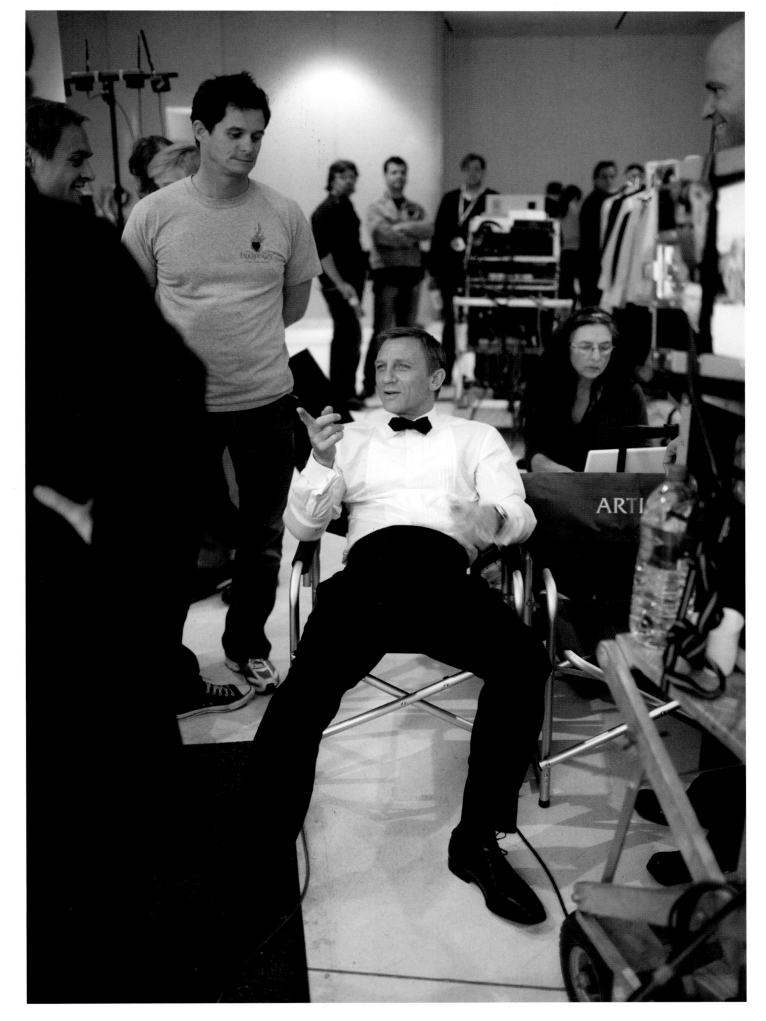

PINEWOOD
ENGLAND

Opposite page and below: Shooting the love scene, between Agent Fields (Gemma Arterton) and Bond (Daniel Craig). This was one of the first scenes Gemma Arterton filmed.

PANAMA CITY
PANAMA

Pages 66 and 67 and right: Olga Kurylenko.

Above: Giancarlo Giannini and Gemma Arterton have fun between takes of the party scene.

Opposite page: Gemma Arterton models Agent Fields' party dress, designed by Prada.

Opposite page: Gemma Arterton studies her script.

Above, clockwise from left: Extras, Mathieu Amalric and Olga Kurylenko take it easy between takes of the fundraiser party.

We arrived in Panama on a chartered Boeing 747 on the 5th of February. The flight itself was quite an experience — then again, what can you expect when an entire film crew is let loose on a plane with unlimited booze? Panama remained home until the 24th of March when we moved on to Chile. The crew was extremely apprehensive about filming in Panama, but any worries soon subsided and everyone realized and appreciated what an incredible place it was. Because the community was so welcoming and embraced us in the warmest way, we were able to experience the most magical of times there. I really loved both the country and its people.

I chose Panama as a location for Colón, a seaport which is on the Atlantic entry point of the Canal. It is often referred to as Panama's second city. Today, Colón is best known for its Free Trade zone. Forty years ago, politically motivated riots shattered the city's municipal palace and the dictatorship of Manuel Noriega marked the beginning of a severe decline. Since then, Colón has been socially and economically spiralling downwards. In previous years, the unemployment rate has reached around 40 per cent with an even larger poverty rate.

What is incredibly special about Colón is its architecture. Many of the city's buildings need to be restored, but, for its architectural treasures, it offers the camera stunning visuals.

Marc Forster

Right: Retired Panamanian boxing champion Roberto Duran with gaffer Eddie Knight and his team of electricians. Left to right: Roy Rowland, Jim Crowther, Dave Moss, Peter Casey, Mark Thomas, Mark Looker, Jamie Knight, Roberto Duran, Ben Knight, Joe Knight, Liam McGill, Eddie Knight.

Right: Daniel Craig, with 2nd assistant director Toby Hefferman and Olga Kurylenko, relaxes between takes.

Opposite page, clockwise from top: Olga Kurylenko as the fiery Camille; Marc Forster directs Fernando Guillén Cuervo (Bolivian chief of police); Camille adds glamour to the fundraising party scene; camera crew Dave Appleby and Will Humphries on a gantry.

Above, clockwise from top left: Giancarlo Giannini as Bond's friend René Mathis; Daniel Craig and Gemma Arterton watch a replay of one of their scenes; Anatole Taubman (on right) with his Elvis stunt double, assistant stunt coordinator Rob Inch; former boxing champion Roberto Duran, visiting the set, poses with Jeffrey Wright, who plays Bond's CIA ally Felix Leiter.

Below left: Marc Forster directs.
Below right: "A" camera operator George Richmond.

Pages 80 and 81: Daniel Craig as James Bond; Mathieu Amalric as Dominic Greene.

Pages 82 and 83: The DC-3's cockpit mounted on a hydraulic ramp. This enables the cockpit to tilt realistically. A blue screen takes the place of sky and desert, which will be added at the editing stage.

Opposite page: Filming scenes set in the DC-3 cockpit with Daniel Craig at the controls and Olga Kurylenko in the co-pilot's seat. The crew member (bottom left) is supervising armourer Joss Skottowe.

Pages 86 and 88 (left to right): "A" camera clapper loader Will Humphries, "A" camera focus puller Chunky Richmond, crane head technician Laurence Edwards, VFX designer Kevin Tod Haug, production designer Dennis Gassner, director Marc Forster, SFX supervisor Chris Corbould, and 1st assistant director Michael Lerman.

The plane sequence was always a big throwback for me. I felt it should have the sense of NORTH BY NORTHWEST, in a beautiful and classic way. The DC-3 itself was difficult to get. We had one in Mexico, where all the aerial combat was shot. We then needed that DC-3 to travel from Northern Mexico to Antofagasta in Chile for Bond and Camille's arrival and take off from the airport in the desert. The Mexican DC-3 was not capable of making the journey due to mechanical concerns. We tried to find a match all over South America but we couldn't locate a single one. Either we couldn't paint the plane the same color to match our existing one, or there were other restrictions.

The producers approached me with a museum piece down in Santiago that they could bring up, but the plane couldn't move and Bond wouldn't be able to take off, but at least it was an answer and there would be a DC-3 standing in the background. At the last possible moment we found a DC-3 out of Miami, which they flew to Antofagasta. Watching that plane take off over the desert, it looked so unreal and beautiful at the same time. I was overjoyed we had settled for nothing less.

The interior of the plane was shot at Pinewood. It was built on a gimble so was able to recreate our flight simulation with controlled and choreographed movements. Shooting that was tough and was a collision between the monotone and the creative.

Marc Forster

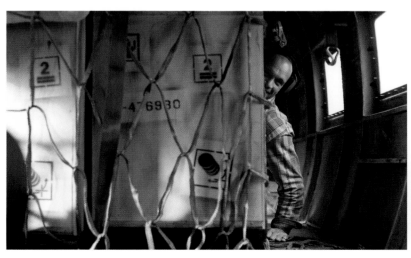

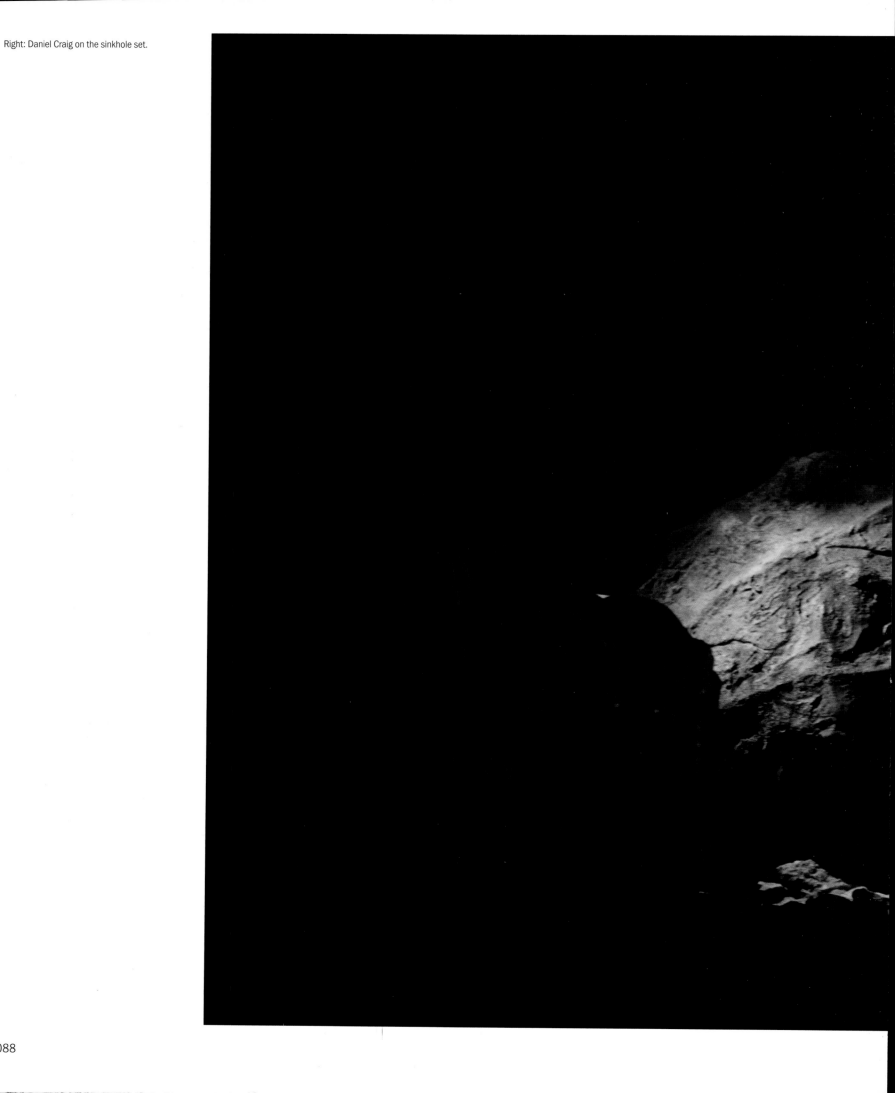

Right: Daniel Craig on the sinkhole set.

Opposite page: 2nd assistant Toby Hefferman holds a door for Olga Kurylenko to escape an explosion. Bottom: Senior SFX technician Paul "Shaggy" Clancy looks at Daniel Craig and Olga Kurylenko laughting at the crew's reaction to their escape from the sinkhole.

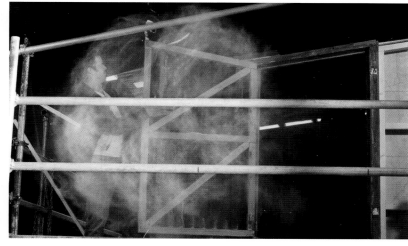

COBIJA
CHILE

Both pages: Filming Bond and Camille's escape across the desert in villages close to Antofagasta.

Above, left to right: Director of photography Roberto Schaefer, camera operator George Richmond and director Marc Forster.

Opposite page: Daniel Craig during a break in filming.

Pages 100 and 101: After crashlanding in the desert, free-falling down a sinkhole and a long, hot walk, Bond and Camille's faces show the strain.

Pages 102 to 105: Daniel Craig rehearses firing a
SIG PR26 (9mm calibre) gun in the Chilean desert.

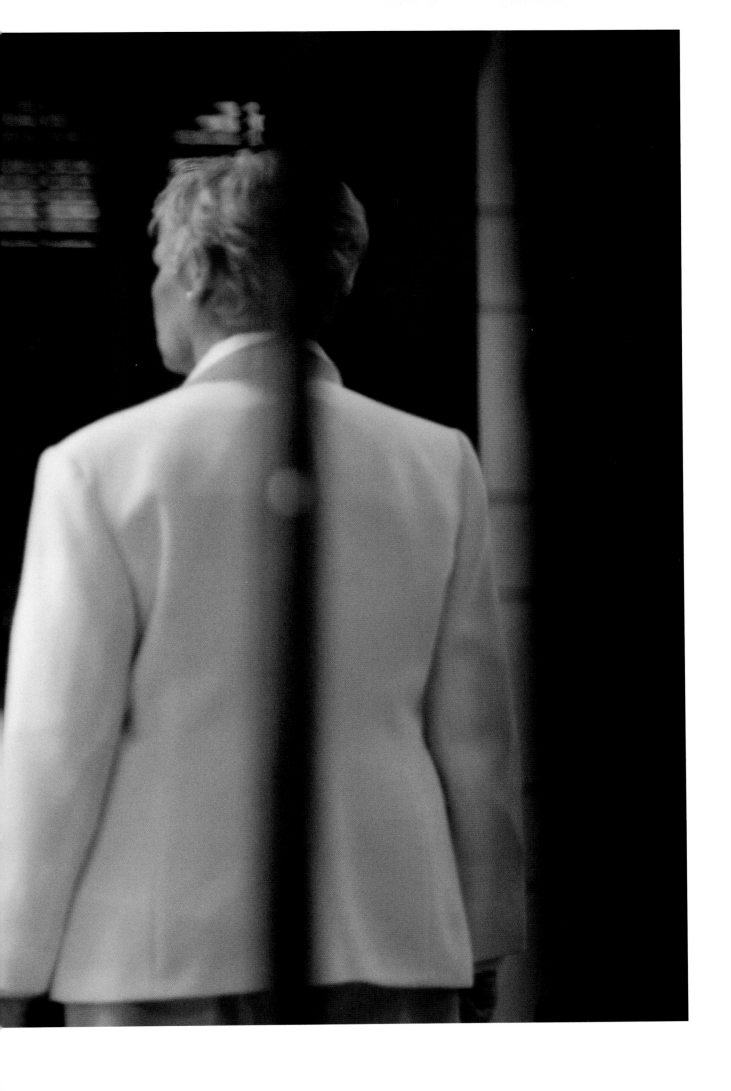

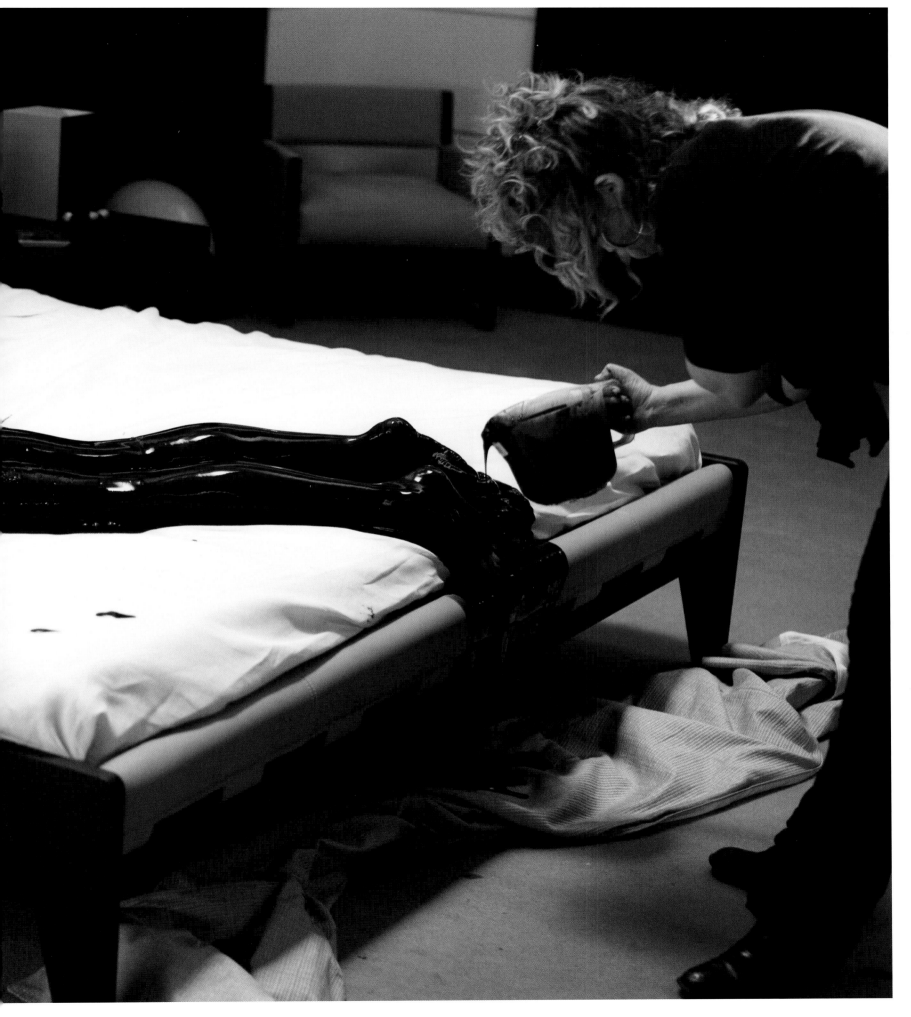

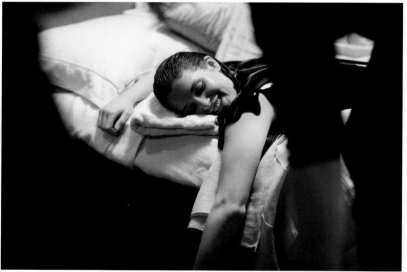

Pages 108, 109, above and opposite: Gemma
Arterton, made up by make-up artist Naomi Donne,
prepares for the filming of Agent Fields' death scene.

Often a homage can be like reheated leftovers, never as good the second time around.
I have paid homage in some of my films, and I enjoy doing them as they remind me
of the glory days of cinema. GOLDFINGER was part of that era, and whenever I get a
chance to reminisce on those glory days, it gives me an incredible joy.

Marc Forster

Left and pages 114 and 115: Olga Kurylenko (Camille) and Joaquín Cosio (General Medrano) and various members of the unit filming the fight sequence at the Perla de las Dunas hotel. Also featured is Oona Chaplin as a hotel receptionist.

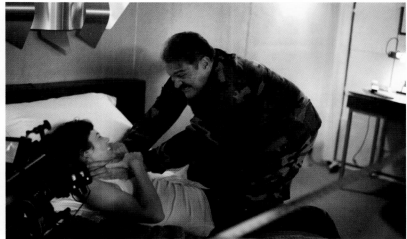

Left: Mathieu Amalric takes cover on the exploding set of the Perla de las Dunas hotel.

Above: The crew set the charges and rehearse the blowing up of the hotel's lobby during Bond and Greene's penultimate confrontation. Lee Morrison (bottom centre), Anatole Taubman's stunt double, cradles a rubber mock-up of Elvis' distinctive visage with its bowl haircut; cameramen George and Chunky Richmond (right) stand ready in flame-retardant suits.

Above: The charges explode on cue in the hotel lobby.

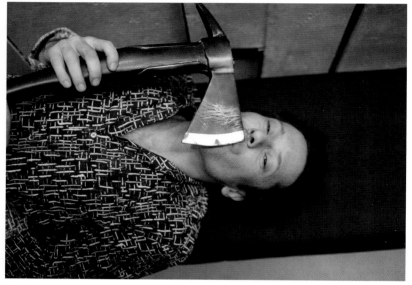
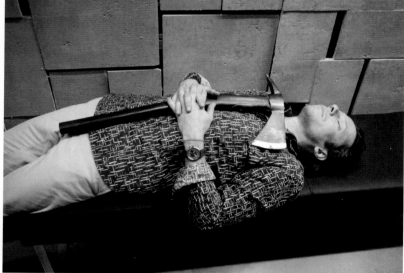

Opposite page and above: Mathieu Amalric
and Daniel Craig film a scene in which Dominic
Greene, his composure in tatters thanks to Bond's
interference, attacks 007 with a fire axe.

Pages 122 and 123: Bond and Greene struggle
while the hotel burns.

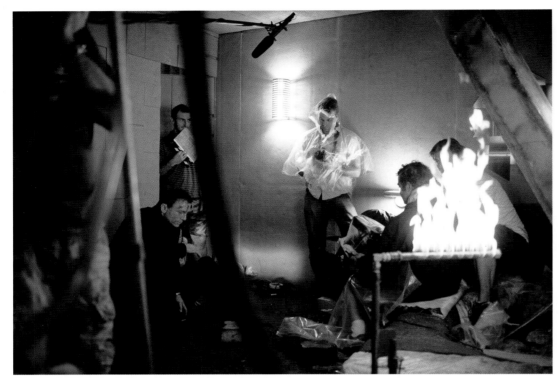

Above: Filming a scene in which Bond and Camille
are trapped in a burning hotel room. Gas jets
generate flames.

Above: Sebastian Barraclough and Chunky
Richmond check camera postion and focus on
Daniel Craig.

Left: Olga Kurylenko and Daniel Craig make their escape from the burning hotel-room set.

131

ATACAMA DESERT CHILE

Pages 132 and 133: On location in the Atacama desert, northern Chile. Situated in the rain shadow of the Andes, the desert is one of the driest places on Earth – no rain has fallen in parts of it for 400 years. The desert is a plateau 244 metres (800 feet) above sea level. The dusty air is consequently thin, and although the sun does not feel particularly hot, it soon burns exposed skin.

Opposite page: One of the problems of film-making in a desert: to preserve the illusion of an empty wasteland, the crew have to sweep the ground to remove their own vehicle tracks.

I'm a child of consumerism, and growing up I realized that actually the less I have, the happier I am. Because of that I'm drawn to simple and stripped down spaces. The Eso is one of those places and feels almost like a futuristic world order fragmented against the surface of Mars. When looking at my movies, the through line of architecture is always similar, no matter what the time period. The idea is always to try to simplify. One could shoot an entire film at Chile's Paranal Observatory and never be bored by what that building offers the lens. Early on I wasn't entirely sure if the emotional core of the scene would play with the right rhythm in a location like Paranal. But the heat and the fire convinced me that, eventually, it would be so out of control that Bond and Camille's connection would be supported through the intensity of the surrounding drama.

Marc Forster

Left: Daniel Craig checks his gun in preparation for a take. Standing by: "A" camera operator George Richmond and script supervisor Nicki Clapp.

Above and opposite: Bond extracts information from Dominic Greene regarding Quantum, the secret organization Greene works for.

Pages 140 and 141: Abandoned in the desert by 007, Greene is forced to follow the tracks left by Bond's car to have any hope of reaching safety.

I discovered my love of the desert in California. For me, there is nothing more liberating than spending several days in the desert, marching into the heat, taking endless hikes, watching the light. Then there's the silence. Embrace it, and it becomes your companion.

I always felt Bond belonged in the desert. In his case, the desert reflects part of his subconscious, namely his solitude and isolation towards the rest of the world. What I find most interesting about Bond, is not necessarily if he is telling the truth or not, but that he is true to himself. If he can bear the accusation of betrayal and not betray his own soul, he is trustworthy.

One of the main underlying themes in the movie is trust. We always look for someone we can trust more than we trust ourselves, maybe because we know how often we betray ourselves. That's the beauty of Bond, his ability to be true to himself no matter what. His emotional dysfunction towards women, which is blanketed by his charm, is still the only existing truth for Bond by which he is able to escape his pain.

Marc Forster

ALDERSHOT
ENGLAND

146

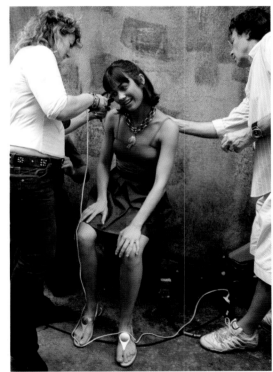

CAST & CREW

James Bond	DANIEL CRAIG
Camille	OLGA KURYLENKO
Dominic Greene	MATHIEU AMALRIC
M	JUDI DENCH
Mathis	GIANCARLO GIANNINI
Agent Fields	GEMMA ARTERTON
Felix Leiter	JEFFREY WRIGHT
Gregg Beam	DAVID HARBOUR
Mr. White	JESPER CHRISTENSEN
Elvis	ANATOLE TAUBMAN
Tanner	RORY KINNEAR
Foreign Secretary	TIM PIGOTT-SMITH
General Medrano	JOAQUÍN COSIO
Colonel of Police	FERNANDO GUILLÉN CUERVO
Lt. Orso	JESÚS OCHOA
Mitchell	GLENN FOSTER
Guy Haines	PAUL RITTER
Yusef	SIMON KASSIANIDES
Corrine	STANA KATIC
Gemma	LUCREZIA LANTE DELLA ROVERE
Mr. Slate	NEIL JACKSON
Pretty Receptionist	OONA CHAPLIN

Marc Forster	DIRECTOR	Paul Engelen	Makeup Supervisor
Michael G. Wilson	PRODUCER	Zoe Tahir	Hairdressing Supervisor
Barbara Broccoli	PRODUCER	Naomi Donne	Bond Girls' Makeup & Hair
		Lindsay Pugh	Costume Supervisor
Paul Haggis	Writer	Eddie Knight	Gaffer
Neal Purvis	Writer	David Appleby	Key Grip
Robert Wade	Writer	Ian Lowe	SFX Floor Supervisor
Anthony Waye	Executive Producer	Katherine McCormack	Unit Publicist
Callum McDougall	Executive Producer	Karen Ballard	Unit Stills Photographer
Andrew Noakes	Associate Producer & Financial Controller	Jenni McMurrie	Product Placement Manager
Gregg Wilson	Assistant Producer	Sean Hill	EPK Cameraman
Dennis Gassner	Production Designer		
Roberto Schaefer A.S.C.	Director of Photography	Shaun O'Dell	2nd Unit Director of Photography
Matt Chessé A.C.E.	Editor	Terry Madden	2nd Unit 1st Assistant Director
Richard Pearson A.C.E.	Editor	Terry Bamber	2nd Unit Production Manager
Louise Frogley	Costume Designer	Peter Notley	2nd Unit SFX Floor Supervisor
David Arnold	Composer	David Cain	2nd Unit, Unit Manager
Dan Bradley	2nd Unit Director	Heather Banta	2nd Unit Publicist
Simon Crane	Additional Unit Director	Susie Allnut	2nd Unit Stills Photographer
Gary Powell	Stunt Coordinator	Judy Britten	2nd Unit Production Coordinator
Chris Corbould	Special Effects Supervisor		
Debbie McWilliams	Casting Director	Jeremy Johns	Production Supervisor
Kate Dowd	Casting Director	Guido Cerasuolo	Line Producer (Italy)
Kevin Tod Haug	Visual Effects Designer	Janine Modder	Production Manager (UK)
Leslie McMinn	Visual Effects Producer	Angus More Gordon	Production Manager (Panama)
MK12	Main Titles	Chris Brock	Production Supervisor (Chile)
		Gianluca Leurini	Production Manager (Italy)
Michael Lerman	1st Assistant Director	Leonhard Gmür	Production Manager (Austria)
George Richmond	'A' Camera Operator	Mike Fantasia	Aerial Unit Production Supervisor (Mexico)
Mark Milsome	'B' Camera Operator	Michael Solinger	Post Production Supervisor
Chris Munro	Production Sound Mixer	David Pinnington	Location Manager (UK)
Eddy Joseph	Supervising Sound Editor	James Grant	Location Manager (Panama)
Nikki Clapp	Script Supervisor	Martin Joy	Location Manager (Panama)
Chris Lowe	Supervising Art Director	Simona Serafini	Location Manager (Italy)
Anna Pinnock	Set Decorator	Daniel Knapp	Location Manager (Austria)
Barry Gibbs	Property Master	Clarissa Newman	Production Coordinator
Stephen Bohan	Construction Manager		
Toby Hefferman	2nd AD	Keith Snelgrove	Director of Product Placement
Ben Dixon	2nd AD	Anne Bennett	Director of Marketing

ACKNOWLEDGMENTS/BIOGRAPHY
Greg Williams

Michael Wilson, Barbara Broccoli and Mark Forster for their kind and insightful words and for having me on their fantastic sets.

Daniel Craig for once again allowing me to shadow him for so much of the year. The fantastic actors and crew members who helped me carry out my work and enjoy times away from home. It is such an honour to work with so many of the world's best.

Anne Bennett for her tireless work and continued support of me.

Jenni McMurrie for all her very hard work making this book happen.

Keith Snelgrove, Stephanie Wenborn, Katherine McCormack and Heather Banta.

Satsuki Mitchell and Laura Symons.

Mike Bone, the great designer of this book, for his hard work, patience and support.

Alex Allan, Alastair Dougall, Lisa Lanzarini and Simon Beecroft from Dorling Kindersley for their hard work getting this book published against such a tight deadline.

Steve Jackson, my right-hand man.

Joe Puleio at Lusso lab in LA for all his great work.

Jim Moffatt, Andree Charalon, Brenda Brown and Jordan MacInnis from Art and Commerce.

My dear Mum and Dad.

Lastly to my darling wife Sarah, and our daughter Peggy for putting up with me being away and caring for me so much when I am back home.

Greg Williams started his career as a photojournalist working in such trouble spots as Burma, Grozny and Sierra Leone in the 1990s.

Greg has shot reportage photographs as a 'specials photographer' on over 100 movie sets and carried out portrait, fashion and advertising assignments world wide for the likes of Esquire, Italian Vogue and Vanity Fair and brands such as Dunhill, Tommy Hilfiger and Lacoste.

Greg has shot posters for some of the world's biggest movies including Casino Royale and Quantum of Solace. This is Greg's fifth book.

Daniel Craig

JAMES BOND WILL RETURN...